PRESENTED TO

BY

ON

Read *With* Me Bible Series

Miracles of the Bible

Illustrated by
Dennis Jones

Edited by
Catherine DeVries

 ZondervanPublishingHouse
Grand Rapids, Michigan

Contents

God Creates
the First Man and Woman

Genesis 2:7, 15, 18, 21–22

Adam was the very first man. The LORD God formed him out of the dust of the ground and breathed the breath of life into him.

God put Adam in the Garden of Eden to work its ground and take care of it. Then God said, "It is not good for the man to be alone. I will make a helper who is just right for him." He caused Adam to fall into a deep sleep. Then he took a rib out of Adam and made a woman from it. The woman's name was Eve.

A Bush That Doesn't Burn Up

Exodus 3:1–2, 7–8, 10

Moses was taking care of a flock of sheep out in the desert. An angel of the LORD appeared to him from inside a burning bush. Moses saw that the bush was on fire. But it didn't burn up. God spoke to him from inside the bush.

The LORD said, "I have seen my people suffer in Egypt. I have heard them cry out because of their slave drivers. I am concerned about their suffering. So I will bring them up out of that land. I will bring them into a good land. So now, go. I am sending you to Pharaoh. I want you to bring the Israelites out of Egypt."

A Staff Turns Into a Snake

Exodus 4:3–5

The LORD told Moses to throw his wooden staff on the ground. When Moses threw the staff on the ground, it turned into a snake. Then the LORD said to Moses, "Reach your hand out. Take the snake by the tail." So he reached out and grabbed hold of the snake. It turned back into a staff. The LORD said, "When my people see this miracle, they will believe that I appeared to you."

Walking Through a Sea on Dry Ground

Exodus 14:8, 15–16, 21–23, 28

Pharaoh and his army were chasing the people of Israel. The LORD said to Moses, "Hold your wooden staff out. Reach your hand out over the Red Sea to part the water."

Moses did as God said. And the people of Israel went through the sea on dry ground. There was a wall of water on their right side and on their left. All of Pharaoh's horses and chariots and horsemen followed them into the sea. But the water flowed back and covered Pharaoh's entire army. Not one of the Egyptians was left.

Manna From Heaven

Exodus 16:3–4, 13–14, 23, 31

The people of Israel were worried they would die of hunger in the desert. The LORD told Moses he would rain down bread from heaven for his people. He said they must go out each day and gather enough bread for that day, except on the Sabbath. The Sabbath is a day of rest.

In the morning the ground around the camp was covered with dew. When the dew was gone, thin flakes appeared on the desert floor. They looked like frost on the ground. The people of Israel called the bread manna. It was white and tasted like wafers that were made with honey.

Water Gushes From a Rock

Exodus 17:1, 5–6

The people of Israel were worried they would not have enough water to drink in the desert. The LORD said to Moses, "Walk on ahead of the people. Take in your hand the wooden staff. Go. I will stand there in front of you by the rock at Mount Horeb. Hit the rock. Then water will come out of it for the people to drink." So Moses hit the rock. And water gushed from it.

18

The Wall of Jericho Falls Down

Joshua 6:1–5, 20

The gates of Jericho were shut tight and guarded closely. No one went out. No one came in. The LORD said to Joshua, "I have handed Jericho over to you. March around the city once with all of your fighting men. In fact, do it for six days. Have seven priests get trumpets that are made out of rams' horns. They must carry them in front of the ark. On the seventh day, march around the city seven times. Have the priests blow the trumpets as you march. When you hear them blow a long blast on the trumpets, have all of the men give a loud shout. The wall of the city will fall down." Joshua did as the LORD commanded. And the wall fell down!

The Sun and Moon Stand Still

Joshua 10:7, 9–10, 12–14

Joshua marched up from Gilgal with his whole army to save the city of Gibeon. He marched all night. He took the attacking armies by surprise. The LORD helped Joshua win the great battle. On that day he asked the LORD to make the sun and moon stand still. The LORD listened to Joshua. The sun and moon didn't move until the nation won the battle over its enemies. The sun stopped in the middle of the sky. It didn't go down for about a full day. There has never been a day like it before or since.

Elijah Goes Up to Heaven

2 Kings 2:11–12

Elijah and Elisha were walking along and talking together. Suddenly a chariot and horses appeared. Fire was all around them. The chariot and horses came between the two men. Then Elijah went up to heaven in a strong wind. Elisha saw it. He cried out to Elijah, "My father! You are like a father to me! You are the true chariots and horsemen of Israel!"

A Widow's Oil Doesn't Run Out

2 Kings 4:1–7

A widow cried out to Elisha for help. She owed a man money but didn't know how to pay the debt. He was coming to take her two boys away as his slaves.

Elisha asked her, "What do you have in your house?" She said, "All I have is a little olive oil." Elisha told her to go around to all of her neighbors and ask them for empty jars. He said she should get as many empty jars as possible. Then he told her to go inside her house, shut the door and pour oil into all of the jars. The woman did as Elisha said. When all of the jars were full and no other jars could be found, the oil stopped flowing. Then Elisha told her, "Go and sell the oil. Pay what you owe. You and your sons can live on what is left."

Elisha Heals Naaman

2 Kings 5:1–5, 9–12, 14

Naaman was commander of the army of the king of Aram. He was a brave soldier. But he had a skin disease. Naaman heard that a man in Israel might be able to heal him. He left for Israel and went to see Elisha, the man of God. Elisha sent a messenger out from his house. He said, "Go. Wash yourself in the Jordan River seven times. Then your skin will be healed."

Naaman was angry. He expected Elisha to wave his hand over his skin. But instead he had to go alone and dip himself in a dirty river! But Naaman did exactly what Elisha told him to do. Then his skin was made pure again.

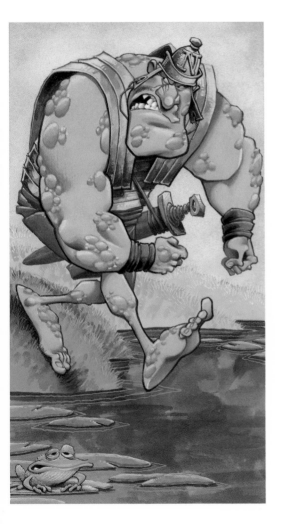

An Ax Blade Floats

2 Kings 6:1–7

Elisha went to the Jordan River with some prophets. When they reached the river, they began to cut down trees so they could build a house. While one of them was cutting a tree down, the iron blade of his ax fell into the water.

Elisha cut a stick and threw it where the blade had fallen. That made the iron blade float!

30

Jonah Is Swallowed by a Fish

Jonah 1:1–4, 11–12, 15, 17; 2:1, 9–10

The LORD told Jonah to go to the city of Nineveh. Its people were sinning and sinning. The LORD told Jonah to preach against sin. But Jonah tried to run away from the LORD. He climbed into a boat and sailed away. But a wild storm came up. Jonah knew it was because God was angry. The sea was getting rougher and rougher. Jonah told the other men on the boat to throw him into the sea.

The men finally listened to Jonah and threw him overboard. Then the stormy sea became calm.

The LORD sent a huge fish to swallow Jonah. And Jonah was inside the fish for three days and three nights. He prayed to the LORD from inside the fish. He thanked God for saving him. The LORD gave the fish a command. And it spit Jonah up onto dry land.

Overflowing Nets of Fish

Luke 5:3–7, 11

Jesus got into a boat that belonged to a fisherman named Simon Peter. From there he taught a crowd of people. When he finished speaking, Jesus said to Simon, "Go out into deep water. Let the nets down so you can catch some fish." Simon answered, "Master, we've worked hard all night and haven't caught anything. But because you say so, I will let down the nets." They caught so many fish that their nets began to break. So they motioned to some other fishermen in another boat to come and help them. They all pulled their boats, overflowing with fish, up on shore. Then they left everything and followed Jesus.

Jesus Heals a Disabled Man

John 5:1–9

Jesus went up to Jerusalem for a Jewish feast. In the city was a pool called Bethesda where a great number of disabled people used to lie down. Among them were those who were blind, those who could not walk, and those who could hardly move.

One person who was there had been disabled for 38 years. Jesus asked him, "Do you want to get well?" The disabled man replied that he didn't have anyone to help him into the pool so he could be healed. Then Jesus said to him, "Get up! Pick up your mat and walk." At once the man was healed.

Jesus Heals a Man With a Twisted Hand

Matthew 12:9–10, 13

Jesus went into a synagogue. A man with a weak and twisted hand was there. Jesus said to the man, "Stretch out your hand." So he stretched it out. It was as good as new, just as good as the other hand.

Jesus Calms a Storm

Luke 8:22–25

Jesus and his disciples got into a boat. As they sailed, Jesus fell asleep. A storm came down on the lake. It was so bad that the boat was about to sink. They were in great danger. The disciples went and woke Jesus up. They said, "Master! Master! We're going to drown!" Then Jesus got up and ordered the wind and the huge waves to stop. The storm quieted down. It was completely calm.

"Where is your faith?" Jesus asked his disciples. They were amazed and full of fear. They asked one another, "Who is this? He commands even the winds and the waves, and they obey him."

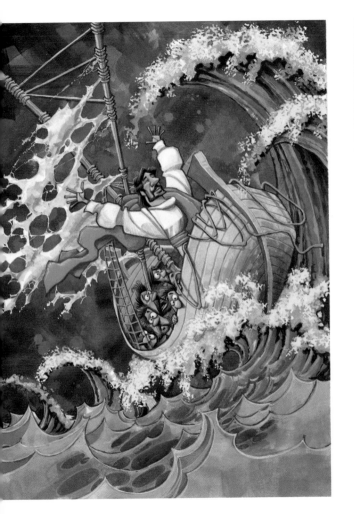

Jesus Heals a Suffering Woman

Mark 5:24–28, 30, 33–34

Jesus and his disciples were on their way to heal a young girl. A large group of people followed. They crowded around Jesus. A woman was there who had a sickness that made her bleed. It had lasted for 12 years. She had suffered a great deal, even though she had gone to many doctors. She had spent all the money she had. But she was getting worse, not better.

She came up behind Jesus and thought, "I just need to touch his clothes. Then I will be healed." Jesus turned around in the crowd. He asked, "Who touched my clothes?" The woman fell at his feet. She was shaking with fear. But she told him the whole truth. He said to her, "Dear woman, your faith has healed you. Go in peace. You are free from your suffering."

Jesus Feeds Over 5,000 People

Matthew 14:15–17, 19–21

After Jesus had been teaching a large crowd of people, he said to the disciples, "Give them something to eat." The disciples said to him, "We have only five loaves of bread and two fish."

Jesus directed the people to sit down on the grass. He took the food, looked up to heaven and gave thanks. He broke the loaves and fish into pieces. All of the people ate and were satisfied. The disciples picked up 12 baskets of leftover pieces. The number of men who ate was about 5,000. Women and children also ate.

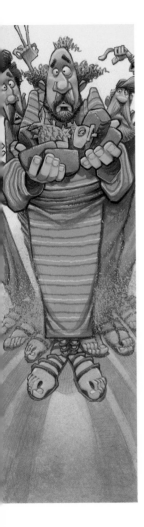

Jesus Walks on Water

John 6:16–21

Jesus' disciples got into a boat and headed across the Sea of Galilee. By now it was dark.

A strong wind was blowing, and the water became rough. The disciples saw Jesus coming toward the boat. He was walking on the water. He said to them, "It is I. Don't be afraid." They took him into the boat and, right away, the boat reached the shore where they were heading.

Jesus Heals a Blind Man

Mark 8:22–25

Jesus and his disciples were in the city of Bethsaida. Some people brought a blind man and begged Jesus to touch him.

Jesus took the blind man by the hand. Then he led him outside the village. He spit on the man's eyes and put his hands on him. "Do you see anything?" Jesus asked. The man looked up. He said, "I see people. They look like trees walking around."

Once more Jesus put his hands on the man's eyes. Then his eyes were opened so that he could see again. He saw everything clearly.

A Coin in a Fish's Mouth

Matthew 17:24–25, 27

Tax collectors came to Peter. They asked him, "Doesn't your teacher pay the temple tax?" Peter replied, "Yes, he does."

Then Jesus said to Peter, "Go to the lake and throw out your fishing line. Take the first fish you catch. Open its mouth. There you will find the exact coin you need. Take it and give it to them for my tax and yours."

Jesus Raises Lazarus From the Dead

John 11:17, 33–35, 41–44

Jesus went to see Mary and Martha. Their brother Lazarus had died four days ago. Jesus saw them crying. He saw other people crying too. Jesus' spirit became very sad. "Where have you put him?" he asked. "Come and see, Lord," they replied.

Jesus sobbed. Then he looked up and said, "Father, I thank you for hearing me. You always hear me. I said this so the people standing here will believe that you sent me." Then he called in a loud voice, "Lazarus, come out!" The dead man came out. His hands and feet were wrapped with strips of linen. A cloth was around his face. Jesus said, "Take off the clothes he was buried in and let him go."

Jesus Heals a Blind Beggar

Luke 18:35–38, 40, 42–43

A blind man was sitting and begging by the side of the road near Jericho. He heard a crowd going by. He asked what was happening. They told him, "Jesus of Nazareth is passing by." So the blind man called out, "Jesus! Son of David! Have mercy on me!"

Jesus stopped. He said to the man, "Receive your sight. Your faith has healed you." Right away the man could see. He followed Jesus, praising God. When all the people saw it, they also praised God.

Jesus Rises From the Dead

Mark 16:9–16

Jesus rose from the dead early on the first day of the week. He appeared first to Mary Magdalene. She told others what she had seen. But they did not believe it. Then Jesus appeared in a different form to two of them. They told others about it. But those who did not see with their own eyes did not believe.

Then Jesus appeared to the Eleven disciples as they were eating. He spoke firmly to them because they had not believed he had risen from the dead. "Go into all the world. Preach the good news to everyone," said Jesus. "Anyone who believes and is baptized will be saved."

Peter Heals a Disabled Beggar

Acts 3:2–4, 6–8

There was a man who could not walk. He had been that way since he was born. Every day someone put him near the temple gate. There he would beg from people going into the temple courtyards.

The disciples Peter and John were about to enter. So the man asked them for money. Peter looked straight at him, and so did John. Then Peter said, "I don't have any silver or gold. But I'll give you what I have. In the name of Jesus Christ of Nazareth, get up and walk." Peter took him by the right hand and helped him up. At once the man's feet and ankles became strong. He jumped to his feet and began to walk. He went with Peter and John into the temple courtyards. He walked and jumped and praised God.

Peter Heals Tabitha

Acts 9:36–40, 42

A believer named Tabitha lived in the city of Joppa. She was always doing good and helping poor people. But she became sick and died. Peter was in a city nearby. Two men went to him. They begged him, "Please come at once!"

When Peter arrived, he was taken upstairs to the room where they had put Tabitha. He sent them all out of the room. Peter got down on his knees and prayed. He turned toward the woman and said, "Tabitha, get up." She opened her eyes. When she saw Peter, she sat up. This became known all over Joppa. And many people believed in the Lord.

Paul Heals Many on Malta

Acts 28:1, 7–9

Paul's ship was wrecked in the sea near the island of Malta. Publius, the chief official on the island, welcomed Paul and his friends to his home.

Publius's father was sick in bed. He suffered from fever and dysentery. So Paul went in to see him. Paul prayed for him. He placed his hands on him and healed him. Then the rest of the sick people on the island came. They too were healed.

Project Management and Editorial: **Catherine DeVries**
Interior Art and Cover Art: **Dennis Jones**
Interior Design: **Sue Vandenberg Koppenol**
Cover Design: **Jody Langley**
Printing: **Quebecor Printing, Kingsport, TN**